THE BRANDING BLUEPRINT

the ultimate guide to creating your brand right the first time

by Christine Arhu

THE BRANDING BLUEPRINT

The Ultimate Guide To Creating A Brand Right The First Time

By Christine Arhu

The Branding Blueprint : The Ultimate Guide To Creating A Brand Right The First Time

Copyright 2017 by Christine Arhu

ISBN-13: 978-1977566676

ISBN-10: 1977566677

Book and Cover design by Posh Brands Co

Published By Create Space

All rights reserved. No part of this publication may be reproduced, distributed, or transmitted in any form or by any means, including photocopying, recording, or other electronic or mechanical methods, except as permitted under Section 107 0r 108 of the 1976 United States Copyright Act, without the prior written permission of the author, except in the case of brief quotations in reviews. Requests to the author for permission should be addressed to to the following email info@poshbrands.co :

Limitation of liability / disclaimer of warranty: While the publisher and author have used their best efforts in preparing this guide and workbook, they make no representations or warranties with respect to the accuracy or completeness if the contents of this document and specifically disclaim any implied warranties of merchantability or fitness for particular purpose. No warranty may be created or extended by sales representatives, promoters, or written sales materials.

The advice and strategies contained herein may not be suitable for your situation. You should consult with a professional where appropriate. Neither the publisher nor author shall be liable for any loss of profit or any other commercial damages, including but not limited to special, incidental, consequential or other damages.
Due to the dynamic nature of the internet, certain links and website information contained in this publication may have changed. The author and publisher make no representations to the current accuracy of the web information shared.

The Branding Blueprint

The Ultimate Guide To Creating A Brand Right The First Time

Table of Contents

01   **FUNDAMENTALS OF BRANDING**

        What is branding

        Personal Brand and Business brand

        The importance of branding

02.   **BUILDING YOUR BRAND (THE BRAND PLAN)**

        Crafting your Mission

        Your core values

        Vision

03.   **BRAND POSITIONING**

        (CPE) Communication, Perception and Experience

        Defining your USP

        Defining your audience

04.   **DESIGNING AND CRAFTING YOUR BRAND**

        Brand Identity/Message

        Brand Design

        Characteristics

        Color theory

        Typography

Table of Contents contd.

- Serif Traditional
- Sans serif: Modern
- Script: Elegance
- Handwritten: Decorative
- Photography

05: TOOLS/RESOURCES
- Pinterest
- Instagram
- Canva
- Photoshop & Illustrator

06: BRAND BOARD DESIGN

07: BRANDING FOR SUCCESS
- Staying consistent
- Creating brand loyalty

08: CONCLUSION

HOW TO USE THIS BOOK

I created this book in sections with assignments at the end of each mini section for you to work on. It's a blueprint for you to follow and work through so you can refer back to it whenever you you get stuck with creating your brand.

Think of this as manual that you get to scribble on as you work your way through creating your brand.

It's also a book that goes into the details of creating a brand and how to go about it without feeling overwhelmed and discouraged. By the end of this workbook, I want you to feel confident in yourself, your brand and in putting yourself out there.

So grab a glass of your favorite drink, light a candle, cozy up on your couch, bed or office and open your mind to the possibilities you can create.

Enjoy!
Christine Arhu

FORWARD

When I was starting out my journey as an entrepreneur, I came across branding and I had no idea what it meant and why I needed it for my business.

After a lot of trial and error, I finally understood that it was more than just my logo. Branding includes strategy, processes and presentation that help deliver your brand in a way that's unique to you and your business.

This book works as a guide and workbook that will walk you through the steps and processes that you need to craft a brand that makes an impact.

The latest buzz word in any industry today is Branding. You'll hear a lot of people say "it's about the brand", "I need to create a brand" or "I'm building my brand". And yet some of them never really know what a Brand or Branding really means.

This one word causes so much confusion that there are about 5000 books on branding alone. Why does it cause so much confusion? It's because like anything in life, it's a trendy or cool word to say.

So that's why I decided on the first chapter of this book, you get to understand what this buzz word actually means.

Chapter 1

FUNDAMENTALS OF BRANDING

WHAT IS BRANDING?

Branding is your businesses or personal reputation. It's what people say about you or your business and the experience you provide your customer.

Branding = Influence

Branding is not what YOU say it is but what others say it is. It is essentially your reputation.

It should be the first thing you think about and develop before starting your business. Because not only does it help in answering what you do, but also helps define the style and design of your business.

Branding is an experience you give your audience through images, feelings, emotions, brand name, style and design.

What is a Brand?

A brand is a promise that you convey every time someone interacts with different facets of your business.

Personal Brand and Business Brand

Your Personal brand is who you are and what you stand for. It is what makes you an expert and defines your strengths and skills. Your personal brand is defined by how authentic you are and how you appear to the world.

Your Business brand is what your business is all about. Who you serve, how you package your expertise, your products or services and what results you bring your ideal client. It's the relationships you build and the strategies you have for building a thriving and successful business.

The two definitely coincide but always be aware of your personal brand. You may have a successful business brand but your personal brand plays a major role in establishing your business.

Branding encompasses ALL of you as a person and business! It's the foundation for your business.

The Importance of Branding

Your brand is the essence of your business. It's what people will remember you by and it's how your business will continue to thrive because of your brand. Branding plays a key and critical role in forming the basis of your business and this guide will help you get it right the first time.

NOTES

Chapter 2

BUILDING YOUR BRAND
(THE BRAND PLAN)

"Branding is not your logo. It's more than that"

Now that we've understood what a brand means and what branding means, let's start creating a plan to build your brand right the first time.

Crafting your Mission

Your why is what fuels your business. It's purpose behind your business. Why do you do what you do? Does it have a cause behind it? Does it help make an impact in someone else's life? Are you building a legacy for children? Or maybe you donate 10% of the profits you earn from your business?

You see, passion alone doesn't cut it nowadays in the entrepreneurial sphere. Neither does making a lot of money to pay down debt a good reason for you to start a business.

With millennials being the biggest demographic of people who buy from small business owners, they also like caused based business that have a strong WHY to attached to the brand.

A formula that you can use to better define your why is

WHAT + WHO = WHY

i do / offer / help / create (WHAT)

For (WHO)

so they / because (WHY)

Use this space to write down words, phrases or sentences that you'd like to use.

BRAND CORE VALUES

What are your core brand values? What do you stand for in life? Use word that best describe what you'd like your ideal client to feel and what YOUR values are. The mesh between the two helps craft a message that will be unique to you and your brand.

From the words below, pick 5 main values your brand stands for then write them in the below. When choosing these words, ask yourself why you've chosen that particular word and what does it stand for in your life.

Abundant	*Calm*	*Crisp*
Adventurous	*Capable*	*Daring*
Atentionate	*Careful*	*Decisive*
Airy	*Caring*	*Dedicated*
Ambitious	*Centered*	*Determined*
Amiable	*Charming*	*Diligent*
Amusing	*Classic*	*Discreet*
Appreciative	*Clear*	*Dynamic*
Artistic	*Colorful*	*Earthy*
Artsy	*Comfortable*	*Easygoing*
Athletic	*Comforting*	*Edgy*
Attentive	*Communicative*	*Elective*
Attractive	*Compassionate*	*Ecient*
Aware	*Content*	*Eortless*
Balanced	*Conscientious*	*Elegant*
Bare	*Conscious*	*Empathetic*
Beautiful	*Conservative*	*Energetic*
Bold	*Considerate*	*Enthusiastic*
Brave	*Conversational*	*Excellent*
Breathable	*Cool*	*Exceptional*
Bright	*Courageous*	*Exciting*
Brilliant	*Cozy*	*Expressive*
Broad-minded	*Creative*	*Extraordinary*

Exuberant	Humorous	Nurturing
Fantastic	Imaginative	Open
Fearless	Impartial	Optimistic
Fiery	Imperfect	Ordered
Fit	Independent	Organized
Flashy	Industrial	Outgoing
Flexible	Informal	Passionate
Flowing	Imperfect	Patient
Forceful	Innovative	Peaceful
Forgiving	Inspiring	Persistent
Formal	Integrity	Pioneering
Frank	Intellectual	Philosophical
Free	Intelligent	Playful
Fresh	Interesting	Plucky
Friendly	Intuitive	Plush
Functional	Inventive	Polite
Funky	Irresistible	Posh
Funny	Joyous	Positive
Generous	Kid-Friendly	Powerful
Gentle	Kind	Practical
Genuine	Light	Pro-active
Glamorous	Light-Hearted	Proper
Good	Loving	Prosperous
Gorgeous	Loyal	Purposeful
Graceful	Lush	Quality
Gracious	Luxury	Quick-witted
Grateful	Magical	Quiet
Grounded	Magnetic	Radiant
Happy	Minimal	Rational
Harmonious	Modest	Regal
Helpful	Modern	Rened
Hip	Musical	Relaxing
Homey	Natural	Reliable
Honest	Neat	Reserved
Hospitable	Neutral	Respectful

Resourceful
Rich
Romantic
Rustic
Seductive
Self-confident
Self-disciplined
Sentimental
Sensible
Sensitive
Serene
Showy
Simple
Sincere
Smiley
Soothing
Sophisticated

Spacious
Sparse
Special
Straightforward
Storied
Strong
Stylish
Successful
Sumptuous
Superb
Supportive
Sure
Sympathetic
Textured
Thoughtful
Timeless
Tough

Trustworthy
Unassuming
Uncluttered
Understanding
Unexpected
Unique
Unpretentious
Versatile
Vibrant
Vintage
Vital
Warm
Warmhearted
Welcoming
Whole
Wild
Witty
Youthful

Your 3 Main Brand Values

YOUR VISION

Like all things in life, your brand needs a vision statement. Your vision statement accompanies your brand core values. It's also a mini business plan of where envision you see your business in the next 3, 5, and years.

Have fun with this because we tend to make the traditional business plan very boring. You can even pull out a board and pin images that you envision for yourself and your business.

Remember it's just vision, a fantasy that you have for your brand. Your vision is not complete without actually take the action to do so.

What does your business want to achieve?

What does your business success look like once you achieve your desired goals?

Your Vision — *Take Action*

Chapter 3
BRAND POSITIONING

In order to build a brand that makes an impact, there are 3 main things you need to consider.

       1. Communication

       2. Perception

       3. Experience

Communication is the way you talk to your audience and where you talk to them. With social media, it's crucial to talk to your audience in away they understand. So using industry lingo with your audience is a no no.

Perception is how your clients perceive your brand and the efforts you make to market your brand. Perception is King. And your audience is the ones who determines whether your brand is yay or nay.

A brand experience is how you live your brand. Your brand is a full on extension of you. It's your lifestyle, your world, and how you live out your brand is how the rest of the world gets to experience it you.

What do you want people to think when they first encounter your brand?

How people perceiving your brand? Are they understanding your message and core values?

How can you build your brand experience around your lifestyle and brand?

DEFINING YOUR UNIQUE SELLING PROPOSITION (USP)

Your USP is unique to you because only you can sell you. Get it? It's what makes your audience choose you and your products instead of someone else a.k.a your competitor.

The notion that you're one of kind should be erased from your thinking. Here me for a second.

For example you're a designer, there are so many other designers out there just like you doing the same thing whether it's branding, web design, interior design or you are a health coach there are so many other people out there in your niche but how you actually package yourself is how you'll be able to stand out within your niche.

Your skills your characteristics your personality this is what creates your USP, so your USP is unique to you. You may be in the same business like everybody else but what you're bringing to the table is different and it's what your audience would be attracted to.

What makes your business unique?

What really inspires you in your business?

What do you want to be known for in your business?

Why should a person buy from you and nobody else?

DEFINING YOUR AUDIENCE

In order to sell to people you need to First Define who your audience is. This is better known as defining your ideal client. So who is your ideal client?

This is where a lot of people get stuck and get confused as to who their ideal client is because they can't figure out who it is or they essentially base their ideal client on an alter ego instead of one particular person who they can market to and talk to really capture them and turn them into a fan. This could even be your neighbor, or family member who has a problem which your business can solve.

Normally how we'll go about defining or identifying your ideal client is by breaking it down into a list of things like (feel free to fill this out!):

Age:

Demographics:

Occupation:

Gender:

Income:

This is just the basic way to identify an ideal client but the way to really really identify the one person who you're trying to talk to who will become your brand ambassador and spread the word about your brand is by really visualizing and seeing this person live in action.

What are the 3 biggest problems they have right now?

What tools, products or services can your business provide to help them with these problems?

NOTES

Chapter 4
DESIGNING & CRAFTING YOUR BRAND

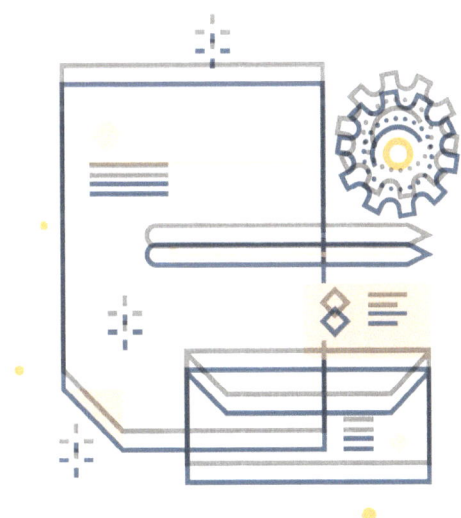

BRAND MESSAGE

Now that we've identified who you are, what you do, what your brand values are, your mission, your vision, your unique selling proposition and also your audience we need now to come and bring all of these elements together and create your bread message before going into the visual design of your brand.

Start with the way you communicate/talk. Are you humorous, quirky, technical? How you talk (and write) helps define your brand message. Your brand voice really helps convey the message, visuals and whatever else you're doing to capture your audience's attention.

Your core values play a big role in shaping your brand message because they're based on your personality and your voice. And your voice is how you speak.

I will tell be the first to tell you to write like how you speak. I mean how else will you able to connect with your audience if you don't use your authentic voice to write to your audience?

What's your writing style?

BRAND DESIGN

Now comes the fun part! Brand design is where most people start with and they end feeling overwhelmed which leads to them re-designing their brands all the time.

Characteristics

Your brand design needs to have 4 characteristics which are

Simple - Easy to read and understand.

Appropriate - Reflects what your business is about.

Versatile - It's not trendy but timeless and can adapt as time changes.

Memorable - Easy to recognize and remember.

Designing with these characteristics in mind will help you really design a brand that get's you noticed fast.

Use pinterest to help you save inspiration from other brands you like. The key here is to you Pinterest for inspiration purposes only and not to copy what you see. This is most helpful when you're working with a designer for them to "get" your vision, they need to see the inspiration behind your brand.

COLOR THEORY

When it comes to creating your brand, the colors you choose convey different emotions for your brand and audience. Also color can be categorized in seasons Fall, Summer, Winter and Spring.

Color plays a big role in connecting your audience to your brand. I can't count the number of times i've bought books because of how the books' cover design attracted me. Or working with someone because they had a color palette that made me connect and get what they do. Color is the main thing everyone focuses on because we are visual people.

Color theory can be broken down into 3 big parts which are;

1. *Primary Colors*
2. *Secondary Colors*
3. *Tertiary Colors*
4. *Color Emotion*

Primary Colors

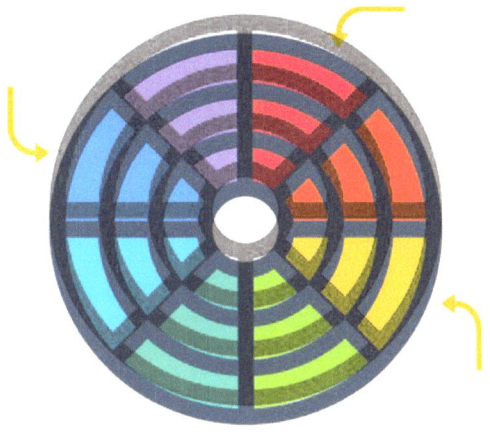

The three colors that make up Primary colors are Red, Blue and Yellow. These are the colors needed to make all colors

Secondary Colors

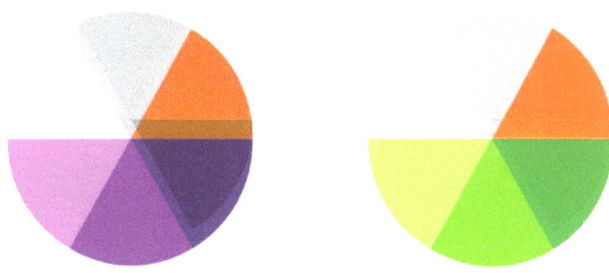

Purple, Green and Orange makeup the secondary colors. They are made by mixing primary colors together.

Tertiary Colors

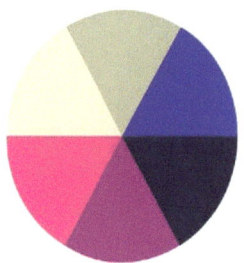 

Tertiary colors are the two-name colors such as red-purple and red orange

Color Emotion

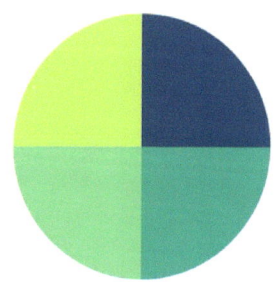

GREEN

Organic, Fresh, Calming, Positive, Growth, Wealth, Life

BLUE

Loyalty, Trust, Peaceful, Calm, Confident, Traditional

Color Emotion

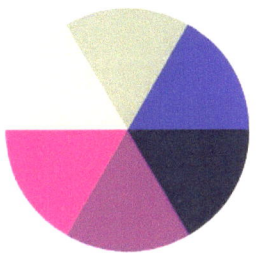 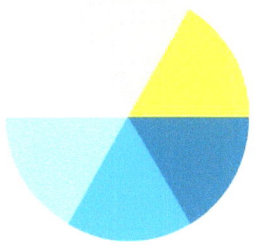

PURPLE

Royalty, Luxury, Wealth, Spiritual, Abundance,

YELLOW

Bright, Joyful, Cheerful, Innovative, Positive

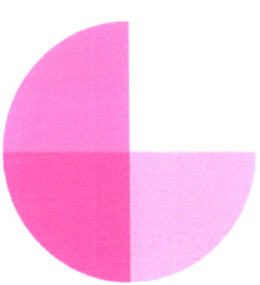

PINK

Soft, Feminine, Playful, Fun, Delicate, High-energy, Gentle, Compassionate

Color Emotion

GREY

Sleek, Stylish, Modern, Cool, Neutral

BLACK

Bold, Classic, Strong, Sober, Stylish, Elegant, Sophisticated, Powerful

Depending on your brand personality and your own personal personality it makes it easier for you to pick colors that compliment each other and truly reflect your brand.

What colors resonate with your brand & why?

TYPOGRAPHY

Fonts tie everything up for your brand. They essentially help you tie up your brand in a pretty little package ready for you to deliver it to the world. But there are some folks who forget how to use the correct fonts in this day and age.

Like any other trend, fonts come and go. As i'm writing this book, what's been trending in the design world are handwritten and script fonts. I must warn you to stay away from trends because trends never stick.

Typography is categorized is into 4 main font types and papyrus is not one of them!

Serif - Is the traditional font that's timeless

Serif

Sans Serif - Is mostly modern and clean

Sans Serif

Script - Is elegant

Script

Handwritten - is unique and decorative

Handwritten

In the beginning of this chapter I wrote about one of the characteristic your brand design needs to have and that's being versatile. Therefore when you're picking fonts for your brand, stick to fonts that are not too trendy and that can adapt to the changes you make as your brand grows.

List of fonts you'd like to use for your brand. For inspiration, checkout Behance.net, Canva.com and Creativemarket.com.

PHOTOGRAPHY

Visuals play a big roll in truly defining the uniqueness of your brand. Having images that incorporate your brand elements like colors, textures and elements really helps solidly your brand from the get go. Especially with social media platforms like Instagram and Facebook where images help capture your audience's attention much faster than text.

There are different ways to go about creating visuals that capture your brand essence. Today I'll talk about 2 main ones.

1, Stock photography

Stock photography are photos that you can either purchase or get for free from different photography sites like Shutterstock, Unsplash, Kaboom Pics, and other sites.

Depending on who your target audience is and what your business is about, using stock images would be the best option to use when you're just starting out.

The only caveat about using stock images is they are not unique. Meaning you may come across a few people using the same image across different platforms.

2: Branded Photography

Hiring a photographer to take branded photos of you or your products will tremendously help elevate your brand, make you stand out and bring the uniqueness that only you can bring.

Also your personality gets to come out in your images and helps your audience connect with you faster.

Going with a brand photographer may be an expensive option but don't let that deter you from getting them done. You can use those photos on your website, social media posts, blog posts, ads and more.

Also think of it as a long term investment to building your brand right the first time.

Chapter 5
TOOLS & RESOURCES

PINTEREST

I talked a little bit about pinterest in Chapter 4 but Pinterest is a search engine just like Google. It's a big database with images that link out to blog posts and articles in the inter-webs. You can find anything and everything on Pinterest.

It's a great tool to use for finding inspiration and crafting a mood board for your brand.

Part of my design process is, I ask clients to create a Pinterest board and pin images that they feel reflect their brands overall look and feel. This helps me as a designer visually see how they'd like their brand elements designed.

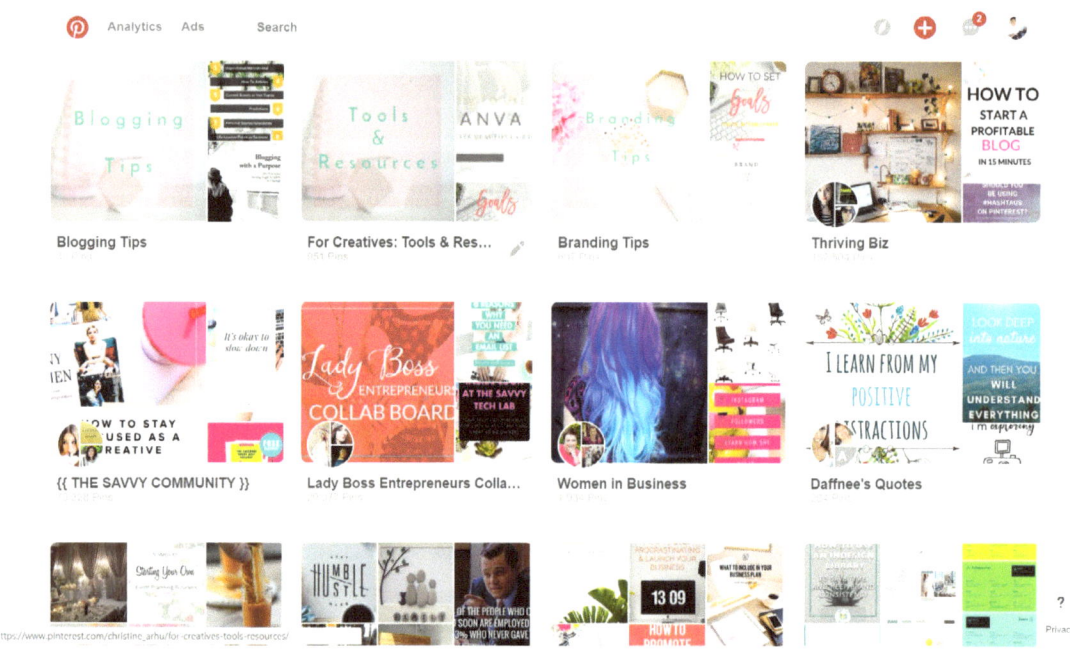

INSTAGRAM

Instagram is all about the visuals. If you're not on instagram, you need to be on it, depending on what your niche is.

Since instagram is visuals, your images or rather what you post need to be consistent and on brand. Meaning your brand colors need to be represented in some form in your images.

Consistency is key when you're building your brand on Instagram and try to create a posting theme that your followers will expect from you.

Calls to action and hashtags are important as well. What would you like your audience to do once they've read your post? Is it sign up for your email list, read your latest blog post, shop your new products, or book a service package? Be specific and tell them what to do.

Use hashtags that are relevant to your niche and ones that your audience is searching for. Using this strategy, you're able to use hashtags that you know your audience is searching for. And ain't no shame in checking out what hashtags your competitors are using either! Be sure to change your hashtags every month to keep up with the relevant and trending tags.

Instagram allows a maxium of 30 hashtags, so be sure and use ALL 30 relevant hashtags to better up your chances for your content to be seen.

Your relevant hashtags

CANVA

Canva is an awesome tool to use if you're technically design challenged. It helps you create graphics for FREE and on the go as well. I recommend this tool only if you're thinking of going the DIYing your brand.

They have templates that you can just go in make the necessary changes you need and they've recently launched Canva Print where by you can print things like business cards, postcards, letter heads, resumes etc.

Check out my YouTube channel where I have tutorials that will help you navigate how to use canva to create your brand.

PHOTOSHOP & ILLUSTRATOR

As a designer, the main tools i use to design branding projects are Photoshop and Illustrator.

I'm a self taught graphic designer and the first time I opened up illustrator and Photoshop, I had no clue, what the pen tool was, or how to upload fonts so I can create logos. So I set out to learn how to use these tools.

I started with downloading templates and recreating them from scratch so i can have an idea as to how the tools worked. Let me just say that i still am learning.

When should you use these tools?

Photoshop - Raster based

- Product mockups
- Photo editing
- 3D images

Illustrator - Vector based

- Logos
- Patterns
- Illustrations
- Icons

BRAND BOARD

I bet you've seen quite a lot of brand boards on Pinterest but didn't know why you needed one. A brand board serves as a guide to help you visually see how your brand looks like over all.

It helps you stay on track so you can be consistent with your brand when you're marketing yourself, collaborating with others and pitching to brands.

Main Logo

Sub-logo

Color Palette

inspiration/Mood

Main Logo

Sub-logo

Color Palette & Hex Codes

#0e112d   #f8b1a0   #dabc7a   #fdf3ed

Mood Board

NOTES

Chapter 6

BRANDING FOR SUCCESS

STAYING CONSISTENT

When you're just starting out, it's hard to stay consistent. I know because when i was just starting out, I changed my brand almost every 3 months! I was confused and I was confusing my audience as well. But the reason I was doing this is because I hadn't identified who my audience was, what made me unique and how I wanted my brand to look and feel.

Consistency breeds expectations that your audience will come to expect. It also helps build your expertise as your audience will come to expect your content, your style of writing, your brand colors, the fonts you use, and the images you use to be consistent.

That's why having a strategy set from the beginning will help you stay consistent. And it's ok to change things up once in awhile. This is called rebranding and you only want to get a rebrand when you're absolutely in need of one.

What are some strategies you can set for yourself to be consistent when you show up with your brand?

CREATING BRAND LOYALTY

When creating brand loyalty, you want your audience to not only to see the consistency, but it's how they experience your brand.

A brand that exercises brand loyalty to the core is Apple. Apple has the most loyal customers and how they do this is through the experience they provide their customers through brand messaging, imagery, and the amazing products they create (being biased here!). This is how cult brands are made.

Building your brand through list building also helps create an experience that's only tailored to your loyal fans. By having exclusive items for them, sending them coupons that only they can use and giving them first access to your products and services will not only create brand loyalty but brand awareness as well, because they will help you market your products or services by telling others about the experience they've had.

What are some ways you can improve your brand experience?

CONCLUSION

Congratulations! You've done the hard part of branding and now you're on the road to launching your brand in no time! You've taken the necessary steps to lay out the foundation of your brand so you can now move on to adding the finishing touches of your brand success with things like a website, marketing collateral, social media templates and more.

Hopefully in my next book, i'll walk you through the process of putting the foundations you've learnt in this book, to launch successfully launch your brand!

RESOURCES

Tools Mentioned:

    Pinterest

    Instagram

    Canva

    Photoshop

    Illustrator

Stock Photography

    Unsplash

    Kaboom Pics

    Shutterstock

ABOUT THE AUTHOR

Christine Arhu is a native of Tanzania, East Africa but she currently lives in Seattle, Washington. She's an entrepreneur and owner of Posh Brands Co. a boutique branding agency which focuses on creating a brand identities and strategies that make an impact for female led businesses.

She has over 6 years design and strategy expertise under her belt and is always excited about the opportunities that entrepreneurship has created for her.

Learn more about Christine by visiting her website www.pshbrands.co and also connect with her on Instagram @poshbrandsandco, Twitter @ChristineArhu and Facebook /poshbrandsco.

NOTES

NOTES

NOTES

NOTES

NOTES

NOTES

NOTES

NOTES

NOTES

NOTES

THE BRANDING BLUEPRINT

The Ultimate Guide To Creating A Brand Right The First Time

By Christine Arhu